©2024 Jami Amerine all rights reserved
P.O. Box 3
Kailua, Hawaii
www.jamiamerine.com

I Can't be a Mermaid Today copyright © 2024 by Jami Amerine. All rights reserved.

No part of this book may be used or reproduced in any manner whatsoever without written permission except in the case of reprints in the context of reviews.

Published by Jami Amerine
www.jamiamerine.com

ISBN: 9798332437366

To the Pixies -
stay wild

I can't be a mermaid today.
For I am much too busy.

And you know...

Mermaids can't chase down cabs,
while running to executive meetings.

They cannot play soccer.

Or dance in the rain.

And their hair is always wet.

The mermaid life might look appealing to some.

But what about girls that love to chase, jump, and run?

I have big dreams and super-grand wishes.

And I will need references from someone...

other than fishes.

I want to travel, draw, paint, read, and grow roses!

I want to taste and see, touch and smell!,

Just think of all the stories I'll tell!

Stories of action, adventure, wonder, and nature.

Oooooo!

Maybe I'll work in politics!

And influence legislature!

Mermaids can't be president.

They can't have a pet puppy, hamster, or cat.

They can't run to town to grab a few things...

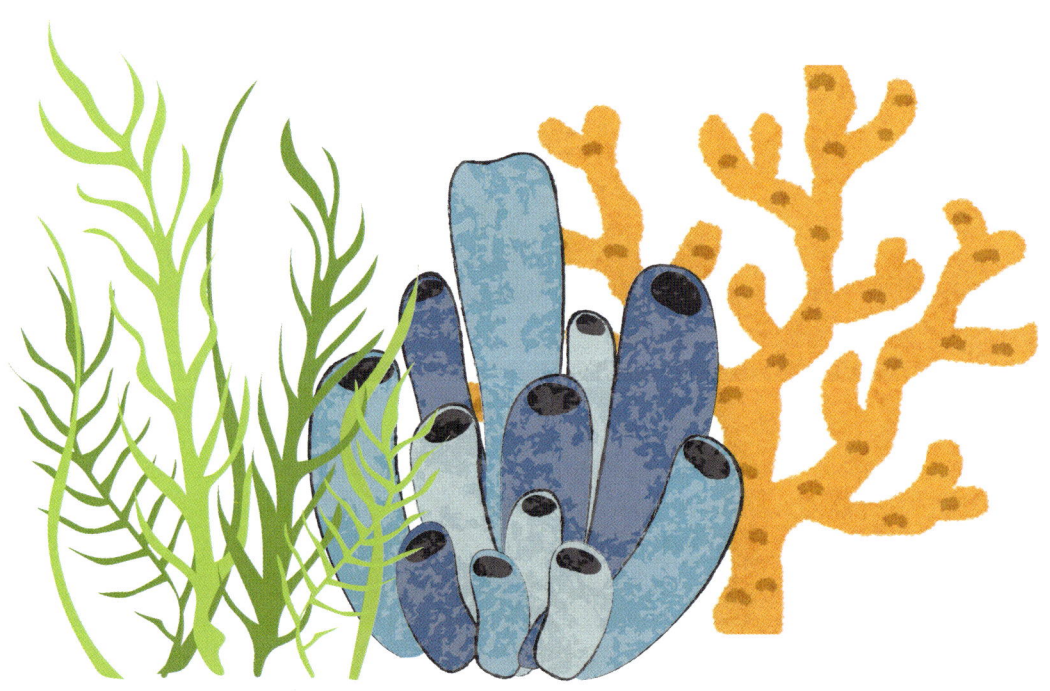

They can't wear a big, fancy hat.

And I promise,
I am not being judgy

But the life I want will require me to study.

Sure, I will study sometimes when I am wet.

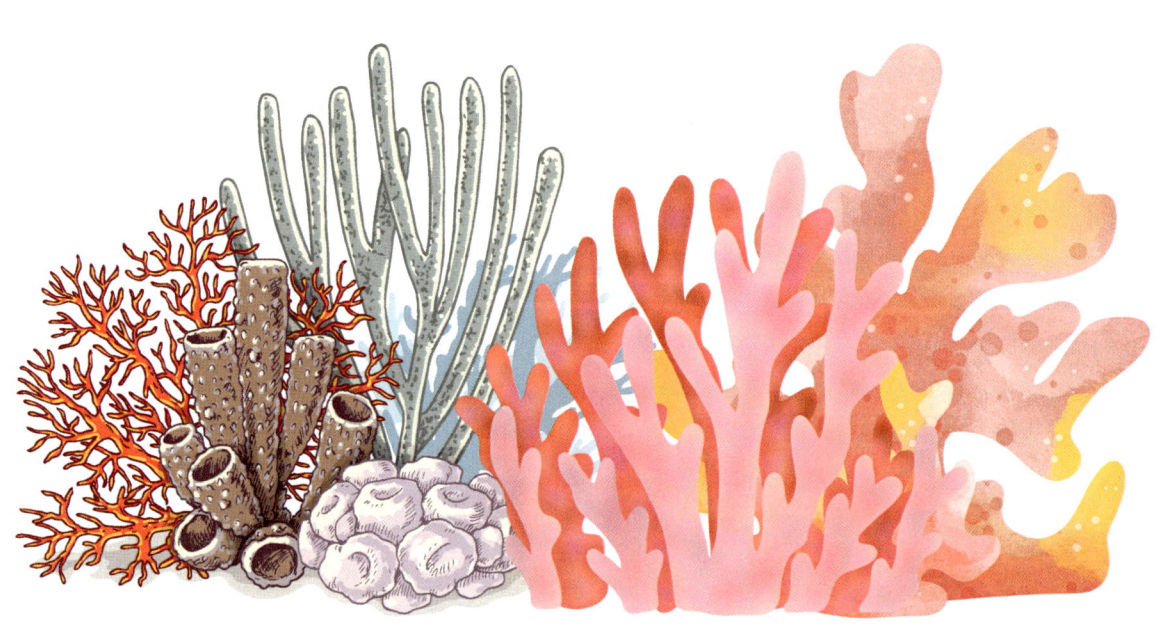

My work ethic will prove
to be a safe bet.

The goals I'm pursuing will require advanced math.

So I may have to study in the shower,
Or bath.

And I get what you're saying,
"Let's all be mermaids and swim!"

But friend,
no feet for great shoes?

Only your fins.

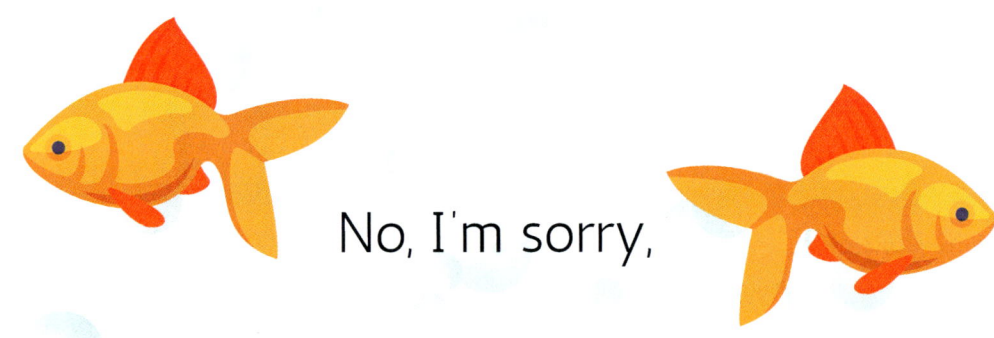

No, I'm sorry,

My corner office would stay but a dream,

If all I did was chase
goldfish and sun beams.

Power sushi lunches would be out of the question.

What if that spicy tuna roll is actually your cousin?

No, I can't be a mermaid.
I don't need that sign.

I am a girl on a mission.

Step back world and watch me shine!

Books by Jami Amerine

jamiamerine.com

"Jesus be all over you!"

FIND ALL OF
Jami Amerine's
BOOKS AND JOURNALS

on

WWW.AMAZON.COM/SHOP/JAMIAMERINE

Find Jami's Art at
www.brushandbloomstudiolab.com

Made in United States
Orlando, FL
12 July 2024